DAVE DUTTON is the author of thirteen books and has written comedy for such major TV stars as The Two Ronnies, Ken Dodd, Dick Emery, Little and Large and many more. He is also a TV actor, having appeared in *Coronation Street, Watching, Emmerdale Farm, Bulman, The Grumbleweeds Show, Flood Tide,* among other shows. His first book of insults – *OUCH!* – proved so successful, he decided to bring out a follow-up – *OUCH! OUCH!* and to join him in the writing has invited LENNY WINDSOR who is Britain's leading 'Comedy Insultant' – a television comedian specialising in taking the mickey out of the audience. The outright winner of TV's *Search For A Star* talent show, Lenny has also appeared in many shows including *The Comedians* – and his own TV spectacular *Windsor at Windsor*. He regularly performs on the QE2.

OUCH! OUCH!

**Dave Dutton
and
Lenny Windsor**

Futura

A Futura Book

First published in Great Britain in 1991 by
Futura Publications
A Division of Macdonald & Co (Publishers) Ltd
London & Sydney

ISBN 0 7088 4980 6

Typeset by Leaper & Gard Ltd, Bristol
Printed and bound in Great Britain by
Mackays of Chatham plc, Chatham, Kent

Futura Publications
A Division of
Little, Brown and Company (UK)
Brettenham House
Lancaster Place
London WC2E 7EN

CONTENTS

Dave and Lenny would like to thank Wendy Wicks for her research.

FOREWORD

What do yuppies, fat men and women, losers, bores, posers, bad dressers, pompous twits, idiots and Torquay have in common...?

They are all on the hit list of this book – *OUCH! OUCH!* – a ready-made compendium of insults for all occasions.

How many times have you been the butt of some wit's pointed remark – and found yourself unable to lash back in the style you fondly imagined yourself capable of doing ...?

We're of the *DO AS YOU WOULD BE DONE BY – BUT DO IT FIRST* philosophy.

To that end, we have compiled this useful cornucopia of caustic cracks designed to tilt the balance in your favour in any verbal pyrotechnics.

Commit a few to memory and go forth secure in the knowledge that you now have nothing to fear from those who would seek to do you down.

With the help of *OUCH! OUCH!*, once you've gained the upper hand, they won't be back for more!

Dave Dutton and Lenny Windsor

PERFECT PUTDOWNS
*(Or, if you can say something nasty about somebody –
say it . . .!)*

If you feel something banging on your head, it's
your brain trying to get in . . .

Excuse me, but when I want to hear an asshole, I'll
fart myself . . .

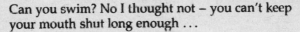

I've seen you on the television – it's called
Interference . . .

Can you swim? No I thought not – you can't keep
your mouth shut long enough . . .

Never mind sonny – there's no school
tomorrow . . .

Who do you work for – British Rail . . .? (anyone
turning up late).

Do they sell those handkerchiefs in *white* too ...?
(dirty hanky).

Mention my name and you'll get a good seat.
(Someone going to the toilet).

No writing on the walls ... (as above).

You're too oversexed – you've rubbed off all your
hair on the bedhead ...

You're as subtle as a turd in a punch bowl ...

You're as funny as a fire in an orphanage ...

You've more chance of getting head-butted by the
Pope than you have of picking up a woman ...

You weren't born, you were *trapped* ... (hairy
man).

You shouldn't be here – it's milking time . . .
(annoying woman).

You remind me of a lavatory – you're always
engaged and full of crap . . . (boastful man).

You remind me of a tampon . . . you're both stuck
up c**ts . . .

If you're happy – why don't you let your face
know . . . ?

The first thing he does when he gets up in the
morning is smile – to get it over with . . .

How do you keep an idiot in suspense? – I'll tell
you next week . . .

If I had a face like yours, I'd teach my arse to
speak . . .

Don't go too near the sea – you'll get a harpoon in
your back . . . (fat person).

It's a pity your father hadn't heard of french letters . . .

It's surprising what you see when you're out without your gun . . .

Why cultivate on your face what grows wild round your arse . . .? (man with beard).

It looks like a sod round a rat-hole . . . (as above).

When you were born, they should have kept the afterbirth and thrown the *baby* away . . .

You've got a brain as big as a fly's left nadger . . .

I'm talking to the organ-grinder – not his monkey . . . (interfering person).

Why don't you keep your mouth shut and give your arse a chance . . .?

Blimey! Who left the cemetery gates open?
(decrepit person).

You look like you've been punched together ...

Isn't it clever how you keep your arsehole between
your ears ...?

Go and stick your head up a dead bear's bum ...

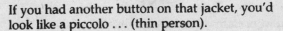

What do you eat for dinner – *growbags* ...? (fat
person).

If you had another button on that jacket, you'd
look like a piccolo ... (thin person).

You seem really hip. I bet you're into the Stones
... How *are* Fred and Barney ...?

Hello Beautiful – No, not *you* Shipwreck ...

Is it true you once went swimming in Lake
Windermere – and left a tidemark ...?

I'm glad you're not scared of heights – 'cos you
won't be reaching any ...

Why don't you go to the Chamber of Horrors?
You'll be less conspicuous there ...

You think you're a big noise – well so is a fart ...

I'm not saying you're fat – but you could go
somewhere as a group ...

I like your hair – did you come here on a
motor-bike ...?

Your hair's short isn't it? – They don't piss about
in prison do they ...

I wouldn't say you look ill – but don't buy any
long-playing records ...

You remind me of the telephone rates – you're cheap after six . . .

You'll never need a brain surgeon – just a chiropodist . . .

No wonder your breath's bad – you're always talking crap . . .

I'm fat and you're ugly – but at least I can go on a diet . . .

You don't frighten me – you couldn't catch me . . .

Your face is your *mis*fortune . . .

They say men who drive big cars are compensating for their small willies. How long have you owned your bus . . . ?

You're so ugly, it would take a beauty salon two hours just to give you an estimate . . .

You've got an IQ less than your willy size . . .

When your IQ hits seventy – *sell* . . .

I was going to do an impression of a pillock – but you beat me to it . . .

Act your age – not your shoe size . . .

You may not be intelligent, but you're stupid . . .

You're not as stupid as you look – no one's THAT stupid . . .

You can light up a room just by leaving it . . .

I hope you live as long as you've made this night seem . . .

With a face like that you should carry an X certificate, not a birth certificate . . .

If I was a lifeguard, I could stop you from drowning – if I took my foot off your head ...

You're the type who stands behind blind people at pelican crossings going: '*BEEP BEEP BEEP BEEP BEEP!*' ...

You're so mean, bet you'd only *lend* a girl one ...

I wish your mother had been on the Pill ...

There's a police amnesty on dangerous weapons – why don't you leave your mouth at the police station ...?

I'm glad to see not everyone has been bitten by the fitness bug, fatso ...

You're the double of Clint Eastwood – you weigh twice as much ...

You're not going to be attacked tonight missis – too many people are into Save the Whale ...

I wouldn't say you were fat mate, but don't buy a whirlpool bath – you'll get poached to death ...

You remind me of my mother-in-law – she's dead ...

I like your girlfriend ... (to man with dog).

You're so ugly, I bet you've been refused sex by an inflatable doll ...

You're so frigid, you'd make a Jaffa orange dry up ...

Your breath could strip paint ...

I'm not saying that you're boring, but compared to your company, digging out old socks is exciting ...

I don't know what makes you tick – but I hope it's a time bomb ...

Stand up and say that! Oh sorry – you *are* standing up ...

The last time I saw a face like yours, Tarzan was feeding it bananas ...

Why don't you start the day with a smile – and get it over with ...?

You're a fun guy – but then so is a mushroom ...

Is that your breath – or have you farted?

I can tell you had no friends when you were a kid – you're still playing with yourself ...

The difference between your mouth and the Royal Mail is that the Royal Mail sometimes goes on strike ...

You grow on me – like a cyst ...

Why don't you take out a timeshare apartment –
in Beirut ...

The Bermuda Triangle's nice at this time of
year ...

If I were in your shoes, I'd polish them ...

What's a rough girl like you doing in a nice place
like this ...?

Why don't you sit on a radiator and warm it
up ...?

There are plenty of fish in the sea – it's a pity
you've no bait to catch them with ...

You'd be a good farmyard impressionist – you
could do all the smells ...

An evening with you is like a ride on the M25 –
the enjoyment is in the leaving ...

Having sex with you is the next best thing to being unemployed . . .

You've got a nose like the surface of Mars . . .

You're the worst example of a man in need of a blowjob that I've ever seen . . .

Good evening Saint George – I see you've brought the Dragon . . .

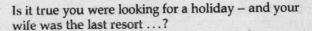

Is it true you were looking for a holiday – and your wife was the last resort . . . ?

That remark was like your hair, lady – not really fair . . .

You thought you were a good lover – till you found out your wife had asthma . . .

I hope your jokes are as funny as your suit . . .

Is it true that your wife is so ugly that at Christmas, you hang *her* upside-down and kiss the mistletoe ... ?

There's nothing wrong with your body – apart from the fact that it's attached to your head ...

You've got a face like an unmade bed ...

I'll drive you home – bend down ...

I think the effect of your modesty pills is wearing off ...

YUPPIES
(The larf's on them . . .)

Yuppies have their passport photos taken out of focus so that the authorities think that they're drunk . . .

A true yuppy puts a condom on his snooker cue to play a safety shot . . .

He's got a map of the U.S.A. – The Actual Size . . .

He broke a mirror and was supposed to get seven years' bad luck – but his lawyer thinks he can get him five . . .

When he needs an enema, he goes water-skiing and mooning at the same time . . .

He was born with a silver spoon up his nose . . .

The Irish yuppy drives a JCB GTI . . .

The new yuppy airline is a 747 Cabriolet . . .

He doesn't want an ordinary dog – so he got an East German Shepherd – it's *very* obedient . . .

He has a good head for money – he's got a slot in the top of it . . .

He's a bilingual illiterate – he can't read in two languages . . .

He's got a telescope for a spy-hole in his Wapping apartment – so he can see who's coming to the door four miles away . . .

He puts champagne on his rice krispies because he likes to hear them go *'Snap, Crackle and Okay ya Hic!'* . . .

Yuppies are such sadists that they buy humidifiers and dehumidifiers and put them in the same room – just to see which one will win . . .

He has red cabbage delivered by Interflora . . .

He won't travel in the same car as his chauffeur . . .

He has designer loo roll . . .

He thinks Greenpeace is a garden vegetable . . .

He filofaxes his f**ks on fax . . .

When he has an orgasm, he shouts out his own name . . .

A yuppy woman's idea of natural childbirth is absolutely no make-up . . .

Statistics show that two out of three mattresses last longer than a yuppy marriage ...

A yuppy always carries a doggy bag – in case his Bimbo gets hungry ...

The middle-aged yuppy wants to be there at the birth of his next girlfriend ...

Then there was the yuppy who had a pre-fire sale ...

He bought a Porsche – then sold it when the ashtrays were full ...

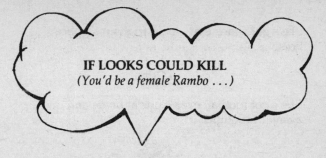

IF LOOKS COULD KILL
(You'd be a female Rambo . . .)

She's got Lebanese looks — a face like a Shi'ite . . .

I'm not saying she's rough, but I wouldn't go out with her even if I was wearing an up and over condom with a zip up the back . . .

I wouldn't say her mouth was big, but she's got a lipstick that only lasts one go . . .

She's got the legs of a teenager — Red Rum . . .

She's got a face like a blistered pisspot . . .

When she takes her teeth out, her vibrator goes limp . . .

She's got a face that would frighten a police horse . . .

She's got football eyes – one at home and one away . . . (Squint).

When she was born, the midwife held her up and smacked her father . . .

She's so fat that when she sits on a moped, you can't hear the engine . . .

When she stands on a diving-board, it *lowers* her into the swimming-pool . . .

She's so big, she puts her knickers on with a Swish rail . . .

She rents her knickers out to Billy Smart's Circus . . .

Her double chin has a double chin . . .

I wouldn't like to stand behind her when she farts ...

When her husband makes love to her, he has to leave a chalk mark to remind himself where he left off ...

She stood on an I SPEAK YOUR WEIGHT machine and it said: 'No coach parties please ...'

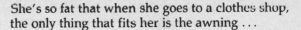

She's so fat that when she goes to a clothes shop, the only thing that fits her is the awning ...

She's so fat that she has to break wind to give her boyfriend a clue where to make love to her ...

What is it? – It's the same shape as a human being ...!

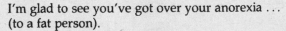

I'm glad to see you've got over your anorexia ... (to a fat person).

I'm not saying that she's masculine but the hairs on her chest go all the way down to her balls ...

She's all fur coat and no knickers ...

I'm not saying she's oversexed, but she's looked at more ceilings than Michelangelo ...

She fancies Ian Botham because she heard that once he gets in, you can't get him out ...

When someone asked her what she thought about sex on the TV, she said: 'It doesn't half hurt your back ...'

She bangs like a lavatory door ...

She can suck you in and blow you out in bubbles ...

She was so oversexed, she came walking down the aisle ...

Her husband once lost 150 lb of fat – then she
came back to him . . .

When she takes her bra off last thing at night, all
the lines drop out of her face . . . (big bust).

She's got a balcony you could do Shakespeare
from . . .

It's nice to see a couple going out together!

When she goes jogging, she gets bruised
kneecaps . . .

She bought a non-stick frying pan – and couldn't
get the label off it . . .

She looks like a bag of shit tied round the middle
with a piece of string . . .

She walks like a ruptured duck . . .

She's a face as long as a gasman's mac ...

She's so small that when she pulls her knickers up, she *blindfolds* herself ...

She's a red-head – no hair, just a red head ...

She looks like a million dollars – all green and crinkly ...

She's so old and wrinkly, she looks like a road-map of London ...

She's so ugly that when she was born, the doctor picked her up and smacked her in the *face* ...

She's only got one tooth – so they call her 'Juanita' ...

Her eyes are so far apart that when she cries, the tears run down her back. (They call it backtearia) ...

She's so ugly, they asked her to use the outside loo on the Jumbo Jet to New York ...

She's a model – for *gargoyles* ...

She's a face like a camel chewing a caramel ...

She's so ugly, her gynaecologist will only examine her by mail ...

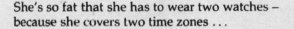

She's so fat that she has to wear two watches – because she covers two time zones ...

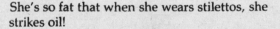

She's so fat that when she wears stilettos, she strikes oil!

She's so greedy that she stands in front of the microwave screaming: 'HURRY UP!'

She's so fat, she has to go through a revolving door in two trips ...

She's got her funeral plot chosen already – it's Yorkshire . . .

She's got a waterbed so big you can get Lake Windermere in it . . .

She can't go swimming in case she gets a harpoon in her back . . .

She wears make-up to make her look prettier. Pity it doesn't work . . .

She lost her husband's credit card, but he didn't report it to the police because whoever has it is spending less than her . . .

Her boyfriends call her 'Hurricane' – because she's no ordinary blow-job . . .

She's so ugly, she has to wear a broad-brimmed hat to stop the birds from shitting on her head . . .

I wouldn't say she's got big tits – I've seen bigger lumps in cocoa ...

She's so ugly that when they're making love her husband puts a paper bag over her head. He puts another one over his head in case hers drops off ...

They call her 'Bubbles' – because she never has a handkerchief ...

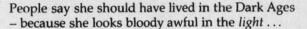

People say she should have lived in the Dark Ages – because she looks bloody awful in the *light* ...

Her boyfriend bought her a pen – but she keeps climbing out of it ...

She had a brain transplant – and the brain rejected her ...

She couldn't understand why she couldn't find the canary – it was there this morning when she hoovered the cage ...

I hear they're putting you on the next space shuttle – to prove a cow *can* jump over the moon . . .

She can't walk through a mattress department in a store without lying down . . .

She's so absent-minded, she didn't recognise herself in the mirror . . .

I wouldn't say she was small, but she got a job as a stripper – jumping out of a sausage roll at a party . . .

She's so thin, I've seen more meat on Good Friday . . .

She loves nature – in spite of what it did to her . . .

She's what you call very odd-looking – six toes on each hand . . .

It's amazing what that one extra chromosome can do ...

Her husband can always tell when she's had an orgasm – she drops her nail-file ...

She has so many lovers, her house has a revolving door ...

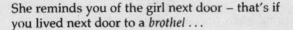

She reminds you of the girl next door – that's if you lived next door to a *brothel* ...

She thought that sucking a Fisherman's Friend was an evening hobby – not a cough sweet ...

I wouldn't say she's got a big mouth, but they wouldn't let her in to see *Jaws* ...

She always confesses to being over the limit at customs, just so she can be strip-searched ...

She bought her knickers from C&A because she thought it meant front and back ...

She thought that the Little Chef was a cook with a small cock ...

She went to see a taxidermist because she heard that he stuffs things and it lasts for ever ...

When she asked her beauty consultant what he could suggest to improve her looks, he recommended a paper bag ...

She could never use a cookery book because every recipe began with 'Take a clean dish ...'

She's got three kids – one of each ...

Her boyfriend said to her: 'Let's make love with the lights on' and she replied: 'You shut that car door – I'm freezing!'

She said to her husband: 'My bum's gone to sleep.' He replied: 'I know – I just heard it snore ...'

She said to her husband on the beach: 'What do you think of my flip flops?' He said: 'For goodness' sake put your bra back on ...'

She wanted to go on a cruise – so her husband sent her to Greenham Common ...

She's the same size as Queen Elizabeth – the *ship* ...

I wouldn't say that she's frigid – but she wears Securicor knickers ...

Her husband only married her because she was a virgin – he wanted someone as tight as him ...

She's so outstandingly ugly that Boy Scouts whistle at her as their good deed for the day ...

A LITTLE HATE MALE
(Men under the microscope . . .)

The difference between him and Red Rum is that with Red Rum, you only get crap from *one* end . . .

His wife has a lot in common with Ronald Reagan. They both married a Nancy . . .

He's just had a charisma by-pass operation . . .

If Van Gogh'd been in his company, he would have cut his other ear off . . .

He recently had his head examined – by a tree surgeon . . .

He scratched his head and got splinters in his fingers . . .

All the lights are on – but there's no one at home . . .

He's got a sixth sense – but none of the other five . . .

He's a brick short of a full load . . .

He once went to a sauna bath – and burned his lips on the ladle . . .

He's a real poser – two cars in the drive – and nothing in the fridge!

He can tell lies – and prove 'em . . .

He's a nasty piece of work – he puts iron filings in his wife's pile ointment . . .

He's always feeding the birds – to the *cat* . . .

His workmates call him *The Lobster* because he always turns up late saying 'One of me nippers is sick . . .'

He went to the same charm school as Hurricane Higgins . . .

You can always tell his house – it's the one with toilet paper on the washing-line . . .

He'll get where water can't . . .

Idle? He thinks manual labour's a Spanish workman . . .

He isn't looking for work – just a job . . .

It's so long since he worked he's got an insurance stamp worth more than a Penny Black . . .

His last job was as a brickie on Hadrian's Wall . . .

His only steady job was as a milk monitor ...

His only ambition is to be a long-distance lorry-driver on the Isle of Man.

He puts down his occupation as 'Zeppelin mender ...'

His job is selling programmes at coronations ...

He rides his bike over cobblestones to knock the ash off his cigarette ...

He smokes a clay pipe because when he drops them and they break, it saves him having to pick them up ...

He's so lazy, he married a pregnant woman ...

He's been going so long to the DHSS, they invite him to their Christmas parties ...

He once got chased by a snail . . .

He's too slow to even catch a cold . . .

He is to hard work what Rudolf Nureyev is to oxy-acetylene welding . . .

You wouldn't click if you sewed castanets to your trousers . . .

The Elephant Man gets more crumpet than you . . .

It has been said that you're the world's greatest lover – and *you're* the one who said it . . .

I'm not saying he's queer, but he cuts his toast up into *sailors* . . .

His cheques don't bounce – they *skip* . . .

Even his coffee's Camp . . .

His hero is the Grand Old Duke of York – because he had 10,000 men and didn't get Aids ...

He's as bent as a deep-sea frog ...

He's so mean that when he had his hip-replacement operation, he asked the surgeon if he could have the bone for his dog ...

He turns his windscreen-wipers off when he drives under bridges ...

He walks on his hands to save shoe-leather ...

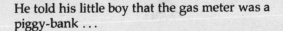

He had double-glazing installed in his house so that the kids can't hear the ice-cream chimes ...

When he plays dominoes in a pub, he's frightened of knocking in case the waiter comes over ...

He told his little boy that the gas meter was a piggy-bank ...

When his little boy asked him for something to play with, he cut holes in his trouser pockets ...

He let a gun off on Christmas Eve – then told the kids that Father Christmas had shot himself ...

When he goes to a pub with his mates, he drinks Whisky and Horlicks, so that by the time it's his round, he's asleep ...

He's too mean to buy a bidet – he does handstands in the shower ...

He dropped a fifty pence piece the other day and when he bent down to pick it up, it hit him on top of the head ...

The only way you'll get a drink out of *him* is to stick two fingers down his throat ...

When he says 'Trust Me' he means 'Screw You' ...

He's as thick as a flak jacket ...

He once broke into his next-door neighbour's to try and gas himself . . .

He enjoys being constipated – because he doesn't like to part with *anything* . . .

He made the Grand Canyon in America when he dropped a ten pence piece down a rabbit-hole . . .

He could peel an orange in his pocket . . .

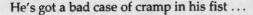

He's got a bad case of cramp in his fist . . .

He throws money about like a man with no arms . . .

When he takes a fiver out of his pocket, the Duke of Wellington blinks at the light . . .

A tramp told him he hadn't had a bite all week – so he *bit* him . . .

He's so mean, he had his pockets sewn up ...

When he throws a party, the beer flows like
glue ...

When it comes to collecting for charity, he's
always the first to put his hand in his pocket – and
keep it there ...

He's so mean, he gargles with mouthwash – then
blows under his armpits ...

He's got long pockets – and very short arms ...

When anyone says that money's made round to go
round, he says it's made flat to pile up ...

He wouldn't buy his kids a football – he made
them use two tortoises having a 69-er ...

He likes the smell of his own farts ... (conceited).

He's more edge than a butcher's saw ...

He's got a head as big as Birkenhead ...

He's got a mouth as big as Plymouth ...

Every time it's his birthday, he sends his parents a congratulations telegram ...

He's got a face that would crack a looking-glass ...

He'd be tall if his feet weren't turned up so far ...

He's not fat – he's just two feet too short for his weight ...

He sings like a lark – a *pillark* ...

He couldn't carry a tune in a bucket ...

He'd pee through somebody's letterbox – then knock on the door to ask how far it went ... (hardfaced).

He's what they call a miracle-worker – when he works, it's a *miracle* ...

He's so boring that deaf people refuse to watch his lips ...

He was an only child – and he still wasn't his parents' favourite ...

He could never get a job as a masseur – he always rubs people up the wrong way ...

His friends call him '144' – because he's *gross* ...

He's so fat, the EEC registered him as a butter mountain ...

He went horse-riding to lose weight – and the horse lost 5½ stone ...

If you lend him a tenner, you'll never see him again – mind you, it's worth the money . . .

I wouldn't say he's got Einstein's brain and Rambo's looks – quite the reverse . . .

You too can have a body like his – if you're not careful . . .

Everybody has a right to be ugly, but he abuses the privilege . . .

He's so tight, he wouldn't spend Christmas . . .

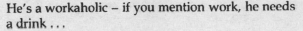

He's a workaholic – if you mention work, he needs a drink . . .

At his house, the dustmen don't collect – they *deliver* . . .

He left his liver to medical science. They're using it to start a rockery . . .

He's such a prig that he once went for a walk and got knocked down by a speedboat ...

His father was in oil – he was a sardine ...

He's a man with all the presence of Lord Lucan ...

He's so sadistic, he bought a contact lens for his dog with a picture of a cat on it – and it ran round in circles for four weeks ...

You can easily spot when he's lying – he opens his mouth ...

He's a coward – he only insults fat people because they can't catch him ...

He's a short-tempered idiot. He had his left testicle removed, went home and gave his wife a right bollocking ...

He's a little shy – with coconuts to match ...

He's all over the place – but so is horse-shit . . .

He's so mean, he went into a card shop and tried
to swap a 'Get Well Soon' card for a 'With
Sympathy' one . . .

He's so crooked, he could hide behind a spiral
staircase . . .

When he gets his teeth into a subject, he normally
leaves them there . . .

He once tried to be flash – and flicked a Tic Tac up
his nose . . .

I wouldn't say he had a big nose, but the reason he
hasn't got a moustache is that nothing will grow in
the shade . . .

He once entered a Robert Redford lookalike
contest and came second – to a Nigerian . . .

He's as camp as a row of tents . . .

When he gets an erection, all the wrinkles come out of his face . . .

He's on his second wife – he lost the first one in a wishing-well . . .

His IQ is so low, he doesn't have children – he *divides* . . .

He has three Shredded Wheat a day – two for his breakfast and one on his head . . .

He never has a hangover – he's *always* drunk . . .

He's done a great deal for the human race – *by not being one* . . .

Drink and sex were the death of him – he couldn't get either, so he shot himself . . .

He died when he got his fingers trapped under a steamroller– he was picking his nose at the time . . .

The reason he isn't circumcised is that he needs somewhere to keep his chewing-gum ...

People call him Quasimodo – because he's always getting his back up ...

People call him Humpty Dumpty – because he's always cracking up ...

People call him Playtex – because he gets on your tits ...

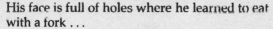

His car had one previous owner – Coco the Clown ...

His face is full of holes where he learned to eat with a fork ...

When he was found in a field making love to a sheep, he told the farmer he'd been having a pee and the sheep had backed onto it ...

His wife's idea of oral sex is to talk him out of it ...

He always wanted to be a Sugar Daddy – but he ended up as a Lollipop Man ...

I'm not saying he has bad acne – but blind men try to read his face ...

He's a Bachelor of Science – and a father of six ...

His mother said her childbirth was painless – until she saw him ...

His wife said that she wanted to sleep on the other side of the bed – so he stuffed her under the mattress ...

He works in films – Kodak films ...

He stopped a child from drowning at the local swimming baths – he took his foot off his head ...

He's what's known as a government artist – he draws the dole ...

He suffers from employment diarrhoea – mention a job to him and he craps himself ...

When he asked his doctor to give him something to make him sweat, he signed him off ...

He's so honest that if he found £500, he wouldn't keep it – he'd spend it ...

The kitchen in his home is so small, he can only use condensed milk ...

When his wife asked him for a mink outfit, he bought her two steel traps and a gun ...

He prefers Fathers' Day – because he says it's like Mothers' Day, only cheaper ...

His idea of a balanced diet is a pint of beer in both hands ...

He took his wife to the seaside but she moaned all the way there – so he let her out of the boot ...

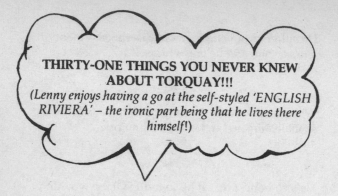

THIRTY-ONE THINGS YOU NEVER KNEW ABOUT TORQUAY!!!
(*Lenny enjoys having a go at the self-styled 'ENGLISH RIVIERA' – the ironic part being that he lives there himself!*)

Torquay's a resort – the *LAST* ...

Saga holidays in Torquay last for twelve months ...!

Torquay has adjusted to the older people living in the town by opening the world's first drive-in funeral parlour ...

The local authorities in Torquay have just brought out the wheelchair clamp ...

I wouldn't say that the funeral directors are busy in Torquay, but they've just invented a microwave oven that seats six ...

I wouldn't say that the funeral directors in Torquay are busy, but they use black Ferrari pickups ...

They don't call it 'GOD'S WAITING ROOM' for nothing ...

In Torquay, the school leaving-age is forty-six ...

I wouldn't say there are many old folk in Torquay, but all the Chinese menus start with the number sixty-five ...

The residents are so old that they don't have sex, so the council now provides 'Feels on Wheels ...'

Torquay has a spring that gushes Grecian 2000 ...

I wouldn't say Torquay is behind the times, but Nissan and Honda have moved out to make room for the Model T Ford Centre ...

Torquay's illuminations were all right – until the bulb burst . . .

They all come out on Tuesdays in Torquay to watch the traffic-lights change . . .

They're so narrow-minded there though that they won't allow red lights on the traffic lights . . .

They used to have a colour problem in Torquay – but he died . . .

Keep Torquay Tidy – eat a seagull a day . . .

Torbay Zoo had to get rid of all its animals to make room for all the white elephants they've acquired . . .

Torquay fancies itself as a posh place so much that in the hotels, room service is ex-directory . . .

The plumbers in Torquay don't make house calls . . .

They make the seagulls fly upside down to stop
them crapping on the old folk ...

They're improving the beach at Torquay – with
quicksand ...

When Torquay couples have sex, they don't come,
they arrive ...

Torquay's youngest residents were having a
pitched battle on the promenade – till the police
confiscated their walking-sticks ...

They won't let you in the sea at Torquay – unless
you have a tie on ...

What's the favourite drink in Torquay hotels?
Embalming fluid on the rocks ...

Torquay's so posh, they make the crabs wear
brogues ...

They have a prostitute problem in Torquay –
finding someone who can still give her one ...

Torquay is known as the pacemaker of all the
resorts – *everyone* wears one ...!

In Torquay theatres, they don't applaud – they
rattle their walking-frames ...

Artists flock to Torquay to paint the still life – in
all the bus shelters ...

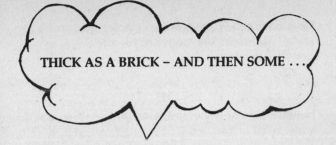

THICK AS A BRICK – AND THEN SOME . . .

How do you get a one-armed idiot out of a tree?
Wave to him . . .

He went to a drive-in movie in a taxi – and it cost
him £96 . . .

He put spot remover on his dog – and now he
can't find him . . .

He went to a dentist – to have a wisdom tooth put
in . . .

He asked someone how long they'd had their
birthmark for . . .

He drove a lorry off Beachy Head to test the
air-brakes . . .

He tried to rob Harrods with a pricing gun and said: 'Give me all the money or I'll mark everything down . . .'

He once bought some powdered water – but didn't know what to add to it . . .

He thinks that if his leg falls asleep during the day, it'll be up all night . . .

He's as thick as pigshit – and twice as nasty . . .

If you combined him with a pig, you'd get thick bacon . . .

When he worked on an oil-rig, he used to throw bread to the helicopters . . .

When his wife had triplets, he went out looking for the two other blokes . . .

When he had a boil on the bum, he kept sticking the plaster on the mirror . . .

He had his house knocked down and rebuilt six inches away to take up the slack in his washing-line ...

When he got a job in the park sweeping leaves, he kept falling out of the trees.

When he found a milk churn in a hedge, he told his wife he'd discovered a cow's nest ...

He bought a parachute that opened on impact ...

He joined the sea scouts – but his tent kept sinking ...

He's so stupid, he loses at solitaire ...

He's so stupid he thought that if he melted dry ice, he could swim without getting wet ...

He bought a three-wheeler to try and beat the wheel clamp ...

He once went for a job as a proof reader for a
sky-writing company ...

When he got a parking ticket, he pleaded
insanity ...

He's got a telephone answering machine with a
tape that plays the engaged signal ...

He's so daft, he once lost a button-hole ...

He had a speed-reading accident – he hit a
bookmark ...

When he saw a sign at the pictures saying
'Children £1.50', he said, 'Give me one girl and
two boys ...'

When he got thrown out of the pictures for taking
his own food in, he moaned, 'Well, I haven't had a
barbecue for ages ...'

When someone asked him if he slept well, he replied, 'No – I made a few mistakes . . .'

He sits in a bathful of water with the shower turned on to find out what it's like in a submarine that's been hit . . .

He's so stupid, he once played poker with tarot cards. He got a full house – and four people died . . .

I wouldn't say that he's a bad driver – but he changes gear with two hands . . .

He pulls out the choke to hang his briefcase on it . . .

When his driving instructor told him to change gear, he put on a different suit . . .

When the instructor told him to check the tyres, he came back and said, 'There's four of them . . .'

When he asked him to let out the clutch, he opened the car door . . .

His right-hand indicator got stuck – and he drove twenty-seven times round a roundabout . . .

They measure his IQ with a micrometer . . .

SARTORIAL SWIPES ...
(Clothes encounters of the Nerd kind ...)

Excuse me – are you wearing that suit for a bet ...?

Congratulate your tailor on his sense of humour ...

Excuse me, there's a bat tearing your throat out ... (someone with a black bow tie).

Is that a shirt or a year-planner ...? (gaudy shirt).

Why did you come out in your pyjama top ...? (striped shirt).

Do you think that style will ever come back in fashion ...?

Who crumples your suits for you . . . ?

His clothes are so shiny that if he ripped the seat of his trousers, he'd get seven years' bad luck . . .

I've seen that suit before – on *All Our Yesterdays* . . .

The only reason he wears winklepickers is so he can tread on the cockroaches in the corner of his kitchen.

She gets so many shoes out of the catalogue, she's got a *club* foot . . .

If she had to send all her clothes back to the catalogue place, she'd be a nudist . . .

That dress looked better in the catalogue – on Lulu . . .

What time do you have to be back in Burton's window?

He's got hairs all over his suit – off his tailor's guide-dog ...

How did you get those trousers on – with a shoe horn ...?

If nobody's died, how come your trousers are at half mast ...?

I like your shirt – do you use it for playing draughts on ...? (loud checks).

I like your jacket – did you get it out of Patrick Moore's dustbin ...?

She's wearing her bingo dress – *Eyes Down, Lookin In* ...

Is that a skirt or is it a pelmet ...?

Where did you get that dress from – Rent a Tent ...?

I've *always* liked that dress of yours . . .

It's the sort of dress that Princess Diana would wear – when there's no one looking . . .

Is it true you wear peep-toe wellies in the summer . . . ?

That's a low-cut gown. If you're going to drown those puppies, I'll have the one with the pink nose . . .

I like your frock – it's amazing what you can do with a bin-liner . . .

I like your shirt. Is it cotton-mix – or just dirt . . . ?

Nice suit. Pity they didn't have it in your size . . .

You're lucky – *Fortunes of War* has brought your clothes back into fashion . . .

I've seen better dressed winos ...

There goes Man from Oxfam ...

His idea of sophistication is to wear a shirt with
sleeves ...

HE: Hi there doll. Can I get you anything – like *excited* . . .

SHE: You couldn't turn a bathtap on . . .

HE: My friends call me The Stallion – 'cos I'm hung like a horse . . .

SHE: I'm going to call you 'Bogie' . . .

HE: Why – because I remind you of the rugged supercool old film star of that name . . .?

SHE: No – because you get up my nose . . .

HE: Would you like to lose two stones of ugly fat . . .? Cut your head off . . .

SHE: Are you breaking those teeth in for Red Rum . . .?

HE: I like your coat darling – did you get underfelt with it . . .?

SHE: I like your suit – I've never seen a pinstriped donkey-jacket before . . .

HE: I love your dress too – was it the last one in the sale . . .?

SHE: You're as interesting as a satellite picture of the weather . . .

HE: Love your hair. Did you have it done at a salon with a glass front . . .? I thought so – they must have seen you coming . . .

SHE: I hope your testicles turn square and fester at the corners . . .

HE: Can I call you Penny? I'd like to come into money . . .

SHE: Mister, the only time you'd have me is when there's a tag on my toe ...

HE: You're small love – I suppose you're what's known as a micro-chick ...

SHE: You're even smaller – you look like you fell off a wedding-cake ...

HE: How would you like nine inches of heaven darling ...?

SHE: Mister, I'm not saying you've got a small willy, but I could suck you off whistling ...!

HOW TO SPOT AN ALL-TIME LOSER ...

He got Lester Piggott to do his VAT returns ...

He bought a camouflage jacket – then couldn't find it ...

He went to a farewell concert – and nobody turned up ...

He wanted to make a comeback – but he hadn't *been* anywhere ...

His father sold kitchen equipment – till they'd no kitchen left ...

He bought a cordless phone – then forgot where he put it ...

He knows when he's going to die – because his birth certificate has an expiry date on it ...

He had the most boring job in the world – cleaning windows on envelopes ...

He said to the tailor – 'I want the cheapest suit in the place ...' The tailor replied: 'You're wearing it ...'

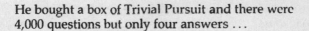

He bought a box of Trivial Pursuit and there were 4,000 questions but only four answers ...

He bought a video recorder and then realised he never watches TV – so it means he's got a £499 lounge clock ...

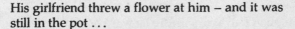

He stole a calendar – and got twelve months ...

His girlfriend threw a flower at him – and it was still in the pot ...

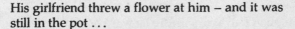

He had a newt that was a teetotaller ...

He couldn't sleep when his wife left him – she took the bed ...!

He found somebody's wage packet – and they'd had four days off sick ...

He lost his pet canary and couldn't understand it – 'cos it was there when he hoovered the cage ...

He paid an acupuncturist 250 guineas to cure him of smoking – and they stuck needles through his cigarettes ...

He knew his dinner was burnt when he saw the chip shop on fire ...

He applied for a job – then found out it was his *own* job he was applying for ...

He was an unwanted baby – he was put up for adoption four years before he was born ...

He caught a cold – but it escaped ...

He took his car to a Jewish garage and asked for it to be Simonised – they took two inches off the exhaust ...

He wanted to be a siamese twin – but his parents split up ...

His auntie died – and in her will, he owed her £300 ...

He lost his virginity at fifteen – then spent the rest of his life trying to find it again ...

He became a plastic surgeon – and *melted* ...

He bought a box of After Eight Mints – and died at a quarter past seven ...!

He broke three fingers shaking hands with a faith-healer ...

He once bought a paper shop – but it blew away ...

He bought a cheap calendar off the market – but it had all the months missing ...

He went to a car boot sale, parked his car the wrong way – and sold the engine ...

He went into hospital to have his tonsils out – and somebody turned the trolley round ...

He caught Aids through standing on a bent nail ...

He went into hospital for a liver transplant – and they gave him Oliver Reed's ...

He screamed when he got knocked down by a mobile library – and got fined for making a noise ...

He suffered badly from insomnia, so he got some sleeping pills – but when he fell asleep, he dreamed he was awake ...

He once had twenty-four hour flu for a month ...

His wife went to the doctor's to be sterilised – and they boiled her for six hours ...

He loves his wife terribly – that's why she screws around ...

Someone bought him some plastic flowers – and they died ...

If Raquel Welch had been his mother, he would have been bottle-fed ...

His father once found a crutch, so he came home and broke his leg ...

He bought a suit with two pairs of trousers – then burnt the jacket ...

He admitted to two murders on his death-bed – then got better ...

He bought his wife a cookery book – and she grilled it ...

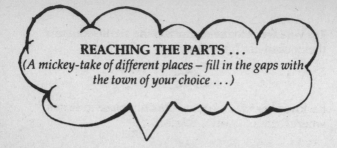

REACHING THE PARTS ...
(A mickey-take of different places – fill in the gaps with the town of your choice ...)

Did you know that *(place of your choice)* has got a new twin town ...? It's Chernobyl ...

If the world had piles, ...'s where they'd be ...

. . . . is such a small town that they only have *one* yellow page ...

... It's so small that the local prostitute is a virgin.

They had to shoot somebody to start a cemetery in
. . . .

... The fire brigade's the local bedwetter

They had to close the local zoo in . . . . . because
the duck died . . .

Backward? . . . . is the only place in Britain
where the motorway's *cobbled* . . .

It's *densely* populated . . .

It's so poor that the locals in . . . . . . think knives
and forks are *jewellery* . . .

They have to sell toilet rolls in . . . . with
instructions for use printed on them!

They have road signs like 'end of roundabout' . . .

You always see people jogging along the streets of
. . . . . . There's a good reason – muggers . . .

If you see anyone holding hands there, it means
they're handcuffed . . .

A lion escaped from the local safari park – and the police were very concerned for it ...

I asked a man with a brick in his hand where he was going and he said: 'To put a deposit on a colour television ...'

. . . . is a great place to come from ... but a bloody awful place to go *to* ...

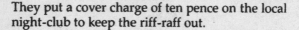

They have a couple of Zulus in . . . . . . doing missionary work ...

They put a cover charge of ten pence on the local night-club to keep the riff-raff out.

Do you know what has an IQ of seventy-five in . . . . ? The entire population put together ...

. . . . is the only place in the country where people leaving their houses wipe their feet before going into the street ...

The one-way system there is so confusing, you
have to throw a six before you can get out . . .

They had to shut the town library in . . . .
because someone nicked both the colouring
books . . .

. . . . is not so much a town – more a morgue
with fairy lights . . .

It's so boring, the locals turn out to watch the
traffic-lights change colours . . .

Vandals broke into . . . . town hall – and
decorated it!

The local pub was so deserted that Lord Lucan
was playing the piano . . .

The theatre was so empty they shot a stag in the
gallery . . .

The local beer's so weak, there's more hops in a dead frog ...

You can drink (local brew) if you don't want to go home smelling of beer ...

It's like making love in a punt – the nearest thing to f***ing water ...!

Don't take the piss out of the beer – there'd be nothing left!

The best thing to come out of .... is the motorway ...

I went to ...... one night and it was *shut* ...

I stayed at ...... for a week one night ...

The Russians dropped an atom bomb on ...... last night – and it did six quid's worth of damage ...

There are some nice drives out of . . . . . . – mind you *any* road is a nice drive out of . . . . . .

Somebody chucked a petrol bomb into a wine bar in . . . . . . – and one of the regulars drank it before it could go off . . .

The IRA were going to blow up the main street of . . . . . . – but they thought somebody had beaten them to it . . .

He has a steady job – he's a window-frame cleaner in . . .

The rent man in . . . . . . actually collected the rent and did a lap of honour – he got mugged on the way round . . .

All the goods in . . . . . shops have *steal-by* dates on them . . .

79

RICHARD HEAD ...

... always wears a condom – but he takes it off
when he needs a pee ...

... has to buy toilet rolls with instructions for use
printed on them ...

... sold his Volvo because he couldn't turn the
sidelights off ...

... thinks BMW stands for Bob Marley and the
Wailers ...

... thinks a maisonette is a small freemason ...

... has an IQ smaller than his neck-size ...

... had a job in an office cleaning the windows on envelopes ...

... lives up a one-way street with a dead end ...

... walked for ten miles looking for his dog – then realised it was behind him ...

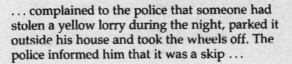

... complained to the police that someone had stolen a yellow lorry during the night, parked it outside his house and took the wheels off. The police informed him that it was a skip ...

... gave himself one off the wrist – and his hand fell asleep ...

... walked into an Army and Navy store in a camouflage jacket – and went missing for a fortnight ...

... phoned Interpol to order some flowers for his mum's birthday ...

... keeps his fly open in case he needs to count to eleven ...

... took his nose apart to see what made it run ...

... married a Chinese woman and when he asked her to do a 69 on their honeymoon, she said, 'There's no way I am cooking you a meal at this time of night ...'

... has so many zits that blind people try to read his face ...

... tried to open a current account in a sperm bank ...

... is going through an identity crisis and an energy crisis at the same time. He doesn't know who he is – and he's too knackered to find out ...

... never gives anyone a piece of his mind – because he's so little left to spare ...

... was asked by his Sunday School teacher to look up Joshua in the Book of Numbers – so he phoned Directory Enquiries ...

... has no flies on him – they all died ...

... confessed to his wife on their honeymoon that he had been to bed with lots of men and she replied: 'So have I ...!'

... was in his car when the wind blew it over. The police said: 'Is this your car?' He replied: 'No – mine's got wheels on the *bottom* ...'

... has designer stubble – on his *head* ...

... had a half-brother and a half-sister – then his mother took the chain-saw off him ...

... makes chips with Cadbury's Smash ...

... put three worms in his mouth because he liked chewing Wrigley's ...

... used to be in amateur dramatics until he misread a stage direction which said: 'Enter, Ophelia from the rear ...'

... drives on the pavement because he's got no road tax ...

... once poked a fire – and it was an electric fire ...

... was asked by a beautiful blonde if he wanted to play around and he replied, 'Why – have you got some golf clubs ...?'

... is so stupid that if he were a turkey, he'd be looking forward to Christmas ...

... won't start a queue because he thinks that the people behind are talking about him ...

... heard there was a flu bug going round – so he locked all the doors and windows ...

... bought his girlfriend a goldfish for her birthday
– then bought a bowl two days later ...

... took three weeks to stuff the turkey at
Christmas – through its beak ...

... made love for the first time last night and was
really frightened – because he was on his own ...

... once thought he had bought a big hamster –
but it was a golden labrador ...

... once waited for half an hour at the bottom step
of some stairs in a store – before he realised it
wasn't an escalator ...

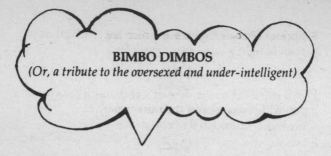

BIMBO DIMBOS
(Or, a tribute to the oversexed and under-intelligent)

A Bimbo has been described as a slag with a press agent . . .

The Bimbo sports model has pull-back ears and fold-back teeth . . .

She was such a slag, even her teddy bear wouldn't sleep with her . . .

She had an internal examination at the doc's and when he finished, forty-two commandos walked out . . .

Her worst nightmare is that Rambo is a poof.

She goes to fancy dress parties dressed as a turkey because she likes to get stuffed . . .

American bimbos say: Have a nice lay ...

When she went to the dentist's and was asked to 'open wide', she kicked the nurse over ...

A Bimbo's favourite town is Cockermouth

Her favourite saying is: 'What a nice night for an evening ...'

The message on her answerphone says: 'Let sleeping dogs lie ...'

I'm not saying she's horny, but she could suck a golf-ball through a twenty-foot hosepipe ...

Her name is Mary – but she's no virgin ...

She can put her tongue so far down your throat, she can tell you what you had for dinner ...

She's been picked up so many times, she's got handles welded to her arse . . .

She doesn't mess about in bed – she's at it before her feet hit the pillow . . .

She's got more fingerprints on her arse than Scotland Yard have on their files . . .

One Bimbo we heard of ended up with seven children of different colours – because she was on Smarties instead of the Pill . . .

The main difference between a Bimbo and the *Titanic* is that we know how many people went down on the *Titanic* . . .

What do a letterbox and a Bimbo have in common? They're always ready with their mouths open . . .

Did you hear about the vegetarian Bimbo . . . She only went out with Swedes . . .

I wouldn't say this Bimbo liked attention, but she went to a funeral and was upset because it wasn't her they were burying ...

She wants next year to be the Year of the Bike ...

Her boyfriend has a twelve-inch cock – but she doesn't use it as a rule ...

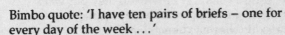

Bimbo quote: 'I have ten pairs of briefs – one for every day of the week ...'

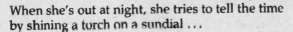

Her favourite meal is a toad in the hole ...

When she's out at night, she tries to tell the time by shining a torch on a sundial ...

When she asks for gingernuts, she doesn't mean biscuits ...

A Bimbo thinks that if you plant a mink in the garden, you get a fur tree ...

When asked what a fluctuation in the stock market was, she said it was a screw with a Chinaman in a farmyard with the animals watching ...

A Bimbo has to take her bra off to count to twelve ...

She occupies her mind by trying to figure out things like: Why is there a sell-by date on sour cream ...? or why there are three people in the Thompson Twins ...? or why do they put walls round cemeteries ...? or when they play Scrabble in Paris, do they use french letters ...?

Bimbo quiz

Q: Who was not pleased at the return of the Prodigal Son?
Bimbo: The fatted calf ...?

Q: Who went to Mount Olive?
Bimbo: Popeye ...?

Q: What was Hitler's first name?
Bimbo: Heil ...?

Q: What are Junipers?
Bimbo: Hebrew children ...?

Q: Name an aquatic mammal ...
Bimbo: A ship's cat ...?

Q: What was Kipling's first name?
Bimbo: That's Ruddy 'ard ...

Q: What do you call a man who mounts and stuffs animals?
Bimbo: A pervert ...

Q: How do you make a hormone?
Bimbo: Don't pay her ...

Q: From where do you get mohair?
Bimbo: A Mo ...?

Q: What were Eve's first words to Adam?
Bimbo: That's a hard one ...!

Q: Name the Dog Star.
Bimbo: Lassie ...

Q: Who were the world's first ice-cream manufacturers?
Bimbo: Walls of Jericho ...

Q: What was Ghandi's first name?
Bimbo: Goosey Goosey?

Q: If we breathe oxygen during the day, what do we breathe at night?
Bimbo: Nitrogen?

OUCH! OUCH! TAKE THAT!!
Jokes that bite back ...

Neighbores ...

Q: Why is *Neighbours* on TV twice a day?
A: Because nobody can ****ing well *believe* it the first time ...!

A bit shy ...

Q: Why don't you see any Jewish Morris Dancers?
A: Because you have to be a *complete* prick to be a Morris Dancer ...!

Ssssssshhhhort back and silence ...

Barber: How would you like your hair cut sir?
Customer: In peace and quiet ...

Black humour ...

1st South African: Did you hear about Archbishop Tutu dying?
2nd South African: I didn't even know he'd been arrested ...

Face facts ...

Mother: I never slept with a man until I married your father – will you be able to say that ...?
Daughter: Not with such a straight face ...

Tongue in cheek ...

Prostitute: You are the vilest, filthiest pervert it has ever been my misfortune to pick up ...
Client: Shut up – and keep a civil tongue in my arse ...

Going down ...

Q: What's the best way of starting up a small business in Britain?
A: Buy a big one – and wait ...

Q: What's the difference between a lavatory and a politician?
A: A lavatory only spouts shit now and again ...

Wife: What are you complaining about? You married me for better or for worse ...
Husband: Well the *worse* is a bloody sight *worse* than I expected ...!

Q: How do you burn an idiot's ear?
A: Phone him when he's ironing ...

What a carry on ...

Nosy neighbour: (to pregnant woman) Are you going to have a baby?
Woman: No – I'm carrying it around for a friend ...

Sick joke ...

Smoker: Do you mind if I smoke?
Diner: Do you mind me being sick?

Milking it . . .

A young smart-arse went into his local Co-op and said: 'Can I have a yard of milk . . . ?

The assistant, thinking he would teach him a lesson, got a pint of milk, poured it along the counter and said, 'There you are, son . . .'

'Thanks' replied the boy, 'Now wrap it . . .'

Q: How do you get a one-armed Irishman out of a tree?
A: Wave to him . . .

Definition of pain: Your body's way of telling you you're on the NHS . . .

Scouch!

What do you call a Scouser in a mansion?
A burglar . . .

What do you call a Scouser in a suit?
The accused . . .

Load of bull . . .

What did Noah do with the giant heap of animal droppings after all that time in the Ark?
Dumped it in the sea – till Columbus discovered it . . .

XXXX

Why do Australians spell their lager with four XXXX's?
Because they're too thick to spell 'piss' . . .

Up the pole . . .

What happened to the guy who bought a German car?
He put it in automatic – and it headed for Poland!

Mod – not mad

Why are there no mods in Northern Ireland?
Would *you* walk round Belfast with a target on your back?

A snip . . .

Why are Jewish men circumcised?
Because Jewish women won't buy anything unless there's ten per cent off . . .

Endless

Why can't you circumcise Iranians?
There's no end to those pricks . . .

Couldn't face it . . .

Wife: Why do you drink so much . . .?
Husband: It's cheaper than sending you to a beauty parlour . . .

Cover-up

Wife: Put your clothes on quick . . .
Husband: Why?
Wife: People will think I married you for your money . . .

Pasta joke

What do you call an Italian with an IQ of 180?
Sicily . . .

Mixed-up

Did you hear about the bloke who took his girlfriend to a foreign restaurant?

She had frogs legs, chicken breast and pork belly – but a lovely personality ...

Roman knows ...

What goes into thirteen twice?
Roman Polanski ...

Caught out

An Irishman was fishing when he heard a deep voice boom: 'THERE ARE NO FISH UNDER THE ICE ...!'

The Irishman trembled and said: 'God – is that you ...?'

'NO,' came the answer. 'IT'S THE ICE-RINK MANAGER ...'

In the swim

Then there was the Irish Olympic swimmer who applied for a job as a bookie's runner in Venice ...

Top ten lies

It's only a cold sore ...
You're the first ...
This won't hurt ...
I've had the operation ...
Of course I'll respect you in the morning ...
I'm on the Pill ...
We'll keep in touch ...
You're the best I've ever had ...
Size isn't everything ...
Of course I won't tell anyone ...

Nose job . . .

'Mummy, Mummy – can I shove this sausage up Grandad's nose?'
'No – and put that coffin lid back on at once . . .'

Bad dream

Did you hear about the politician who dreamed he was in the House of Lords.
When he woke up – HE WAS . . .!

Cut . . .

He: Do you file your nails after you've cut them?
She: No, you dickhead, I throw them away . . .

Eye eye . . .

He: What lovely lips you've got . . .
She: Maybe – but please take your knees out of my eyes . . .

Eye eye eye . . .

Doctor: I'm afraid you're pregnant miss.
Girl: I can't be – we only made love with our eyes . . .
Doctor: Well somebody's cockeyed . . .

Lick that!

Wife: What would you say if I told you I was having it off with your best friend?
Husband: I'd say you were a lesbian . . .

Of course . . .

What's the difference between looking for a lost golf ball and a mounted policeman?
Looking for a lost golf ball is a hunt on a course . . .

Gospel truth

The tub-thumping travelling evangelist approached the beautiful blonde receptionist at the hotel where he was staying and invited her up to his room.

Intrigued by this interest from such a religious man, she took up his invitation after she finished work and was amazed to see him take off his trousers as soon as she walked into the room.

'Get in the bed, my dear . . .' he urged.

'But are you sure this is right?' she protested. 'After all, you are a Man of God . . .'

'Fear not,' said the preacher. 'For it is written in the Bible . . .'

'Oh well, if it's written in the Bible, it must be all right' said the blonde, meekly obeying his request.

They made wild, passionate love all through the night, pausing only for her to be reassured by the preacher that 'It is written in the Bible . . .'

The following morning, as she prepared to leave his room, she said: 'Before I go, will you show me exactly where it is written in the Bible . . . ?'

'Certainly my dear,' smiled the evangelist – and opened the Gideon's Bible on his bedside table to the flyleaf where a previous guest had written: 'THE DUMB BLONDE RECEPTIONIST SCREWS LIKE A BUNNY RABBIT!'

Slowcoaches

Why are people who practice coitus interruptus like British Rail trains?
They never usually pull out on time . . .

Different ball game . . .

The couple were in the threshings of a frantic
lovemaking bout when suddenly, the husband
yelled out: 'Open your legs . . . wider, wider . . .'

'What are you trying to do – get your balls in as
well?' she snarled.

'No stupid' he replied. 'I'm trying to get them
out . . .!'

Ah so it is . . .

What's 200 yards long with an arsehole on either
side?
A radar trap . . .

Baah!

What's the best-selling line in Welsh sex shops?
Blow-up sheep . . .

No charge

He: Do you believe in free love?
She: Have I ever given you a bill . . .?

Sauce!

On their wedding night, the young couple were
disrobing for bed when the bride suddenly
smacked the groom across the face . . .

'What's *THAT* for?' he wailed, rubbing his
smarting face.

'For having such a little dick,' snarled the bride.

The husband drew back his arm and knocked
his spouse clean out of bed.

'And what's *THAT* for?' she cried.

'Knowing the ****ing difference!' replied the
groom.

Ewe what?

The Welsh shepherd sat down to his tea one day to be served by his wife with a plateful of grass.

'And what do you call *this*?' he angrily remonstrated.

'Get it down you,' replied his wife. 'If it's good enough for your fancy woman, it's good enough for you ...'

Dick Tater ...

'Tell me,' said the young Irishman to his friend on holiday. 'How come you're so popular with all the girls, while they just seem to ignore me completely ...?'

'I'll let you into my secret,' said his mate. 'When I go swimming, I always stick a potato down my trunks to accentuate my masculinity. The girls don't half find it a turn-on ...'

'Bejazers I'll try that!' exclaimed the Irish lad ... and rushed away eagerly.

Next day, he collared his friend by the side of the pool and moaned: 'Here, I want a word with you – I thought you said that if I put a potato down my trunks the girls would flock around me – but all they do now is run away ...'

'Yes,' said his friend. 'But you see Seamus, you're supposed to put the potato down the *front* of your trunks!'

Come again?

Husband: Darling, I've been thinking about our sex life and one thing puzzles me.
Wife: What's that darling?
Husband: How come you never tell me when you've had an orgasm?
Wife: You're never there ...

Going gone . . .

The colonel's wife was appearing in the Divorce Court, cited by her husband on the grounds of adultery with the entire regiment.

'According to your husband,' said the judge peering at her over his half-moon spectacles, 'you are nothing but a raving nymphomaniac. Is that so, madam?'

'How dare he say that!' she replied. 'I refute the allegation most strongly!'

'In that case,' said the judge, 'May I have my gavel back . . . ?'

Mates

Coming home early from work one night, the husband found his wife in bed with his best friend.

'Charlie – how could you? I *have* to . . .'

Quackers

How can you tell an Irishman at a cock-fight?
He's the one with the duck . . .

How can you tell if the Mafia are at the cock-fight?
The duck wins . . .

Up the workers . . .

Why are bosses like nappies?
Because they're always on your arse and they're full of shit . . .

Tactless . . .

Wife: Will you still love me when I'm old and grey?
Husband: Of course I do . . .

Not so daft ...

Two Englishmen decided to take the mickey out of an Irish barman.

The first one went up to him and said: 'Saint Patrick was a pillock ...'

The barman didn't bat an eyelid – he just carried on cleaning the beer glasses.

The other Englishman went up to him and said: 'Saint Patrick was an Englishman ...'

'*Oi know – yer mate just told me ...*' was the sardonic reply.

Screwy

Buxom Betty went up to the man behind the counter of the local hardware store and asked:

'Will you give me a screw for my cupboard door?'

'Certainly,' he replied. 'And if you're any good, I'll take you out for a meal after too ...'

Drop it

Woman: How much would it cost to have my face lifted?

Plastic Surgeon: Let me put it this way madam – it would be a lot cheaper to have your body lowered ...

Sweet talk

The little boy had been asking his mother where he came from. She told him that he was a sweet little thing who had been born in a sugar bowl. He sought to verify the information with his father.

Boy: Mum says I came out of a sugar bowl ...

Dad: That's about the size of it son ...

Inflation

The young man went into the doctor's surgery and intimated that there was something wrong with his wedding tackle.

The doc ordered him to drop his trousers which he did – revealing the minutest of penises. It was a short stubby apology for a dong, no bigger than the tip of your little finger.

On seeing it, the doctor burst into fits of laughter, unable to contain himself.

Clutching his sides, he sank to the floor, helpless with mirth, to the acute embarrassment of the patient.

Eventually, after a long struggle, he managed to regain control of himself.

Doctor: (shamefaced) I do apologise for that unwonted behaviour but I just couldn't help it. To tell you the truth, I've never seen anything like it before. Now then, what seems to be the trouble . . . ?

Patient: (bursting into tears) It's *swollen* . . .

Open for business

'I had a funny dream last night,' said the likely lad to his live-in girlfriend.

'I dreamt that they were auctioning ladies' parts off. There were cute little rosebud ones for £200, bigger ones for £100 and even bigger ones still for £25 . . .'

'What about one like mine . . . ?' she enquired sweetly.

'That's what they were holding the auction in,' came the reply . . .

Touch titty

He had a hump, a big nose, buck teeth, one leg shorter than the other, sticky-out ears and thick lips. Not surprisingly, he could not get a girl.

One night, he prayed: 'Please God, send me some money then I can have plastic surgery and look like everyone else ...'

To his surprise a voice from above boomed: 'IT SHALL BE DONE MY SON ...'

Not long after, to his amazement, he won £75,000 on the football pools and arranged immediately to go into hospital to have the plastic surgery carried out.

It was an amazing transformation ... He now looked like a cross between Robert Redford and Sylvester Stallone ...

As he strode whistling happily out of hospital, he took an admiring glance at himself in a shop window.

Just then, a bus mounted the pavement and killed him.

When he got to Heaven, he marched straight up to God and wailed: 'Why did you have to take me just after I'd got my face fixed and all ...?'

'SORRY', said God. 'BUT I DIDN'T RECOGNISE YOU ...!'

Collared ...

Young boy in gents' outfitters: I want a shirt for my dad's birthday.
Shop-owner: Something like the one I'm wearing?
Boy: No – he wants a *clean* one ...

Going ape

The young mother was in tears. She had been feeding her baby on the train when a crowd of soccer hooligans suddenly burst into the compartment and started poking fun at the offspring – comparing it unfavourably to a chimpanzee.

Rescue came in the unlikely shape of a City gent who chased the yobs away with his rolled umbrella and set about comforting the distressed damsel.

'Don't cry my dear – here, have one of my sandwiches,' he cooed ...

'And see – here's a banana for your monkey ...'

Spitting image

Why do Italian boys have moustaches?
So they can look like their mothers ...

Look ewe

What do you call a Welshman with 700 girlfriends?
A shepherd ...

Welsh dragon

Englishman: I only know two things about Wales. One is that they have some good rugby players and the other is that they have the ugliest women in the world ...
Second Man: I'll have you know that my wife is from Wales ...
Englishman: Really – what position does she play ...?

Dead funny

What's the difference between an Irish wedding and an Irish funeral?
One less drunk!

Sourpuss

Two men were discussing which of them had the ugliest wife ...

The first one said – 'My wife is so fat that she has her own postcode ...'

The second said: 'That's nothing – mine is so ugly that when she puts cold cream on her face it *curdles* ...'

Irish knock knock joke

'Who's there?'
'Knock Knock!'

True

'Mummy, Mummy – do prostitutes have babies?'
'Of course they do darling – where do you think traffic wardens come from ...?'

Lay on words ...

The Women's Lib meeting was at fever pitch.

'I want you all to remember that women were the foundation of the nation,' shouted the madam chairperson.

'Yes,' replied a gruff voice at the back of the hall, 'but just remember who laid the foundations ...'

By gum

What's got eighty-eight legs and twelve teeth?
The front row at a Max Bygraves concert ...

A real choker

How do Scottish suicides save money on the price
of a rope?
They hang from the rafters with one hand and
throttle themselves with the other.

Dicktator

What do you call a man with eleven dicks?
– Graham Gooch

W*nker

What happened to the Irishman who entered a
masturbation competition?
He came nowhere ...

Did you know that Frank Ifield and Johnny Rotten
have made a new record together?
It's called: '*I Remember You – You Dickhead* ...'

CAR JOKES ... (due to legal reasons – insert your
own make of car ...!)

What do you call an open-top *****?
A skip ...

How do you double the weight of a *****?
Paint it ...

What do you call a ***** with twin exhausts?
A wheelbarrow ...

Why do *****'s have heated rear windows?
To keep your hands warm while you're pushing
it ...

How do you double the value of a *****?
Fill it with petrol ...

Which ***** will last for 20 years?
The one with 'Matchbox' written on the bottom ...

What happened when a ***** hit a rabbit in the
middle of the road?
The rabbit was okay – but the car was a
write-off ...

Chelsea Football Club promised their players a
***** each if they won the next game.
They lost 28–nil ...